The Silent World
That Won't Stop Talking

ACKNOWLEDGEMENT

I acknowledge the Woi Wurrung and Boon Wurrung language groups of the Eastern Kulin Nations on whose stolen lands I live, work and create. I pay my respects to their Ancestors and Elders, past and present. Indigenous sovereignty was never ceded.

Copyright © Nico Lim 2021
All rights reserved.

Naarm, Australia

Illustrations by Rose Clark
Poetry by Nico Lim

ISBN 9780645384406

www.instagram.com/_flashpoetry
flashpoetryproject@gmail.com

In collaboration with Black Spark
235A St Georges Rd, Northcote
Melbourne, VIC 3070

THE SILENT WORLD
THAT WON'T STOP TALKING

Poetry

———————————

Nico

 @_flashpoetry

FOR NEW POETRY READERS

For those new to poetry, a single piece
of advice will serve you: Take your time.

*"You cannot read a poem too slowly,
but you can certainly read one too fast."*

Meeting these poems halfway with your
own ponderings & interpretations will
let you reap the most from these pages.

CONTENTS

NEW WORLDS REMAIN   1

Beneath the Starry Sky	4
Other Roads	5
The World Grows with You	6
But One Life	7
When You Arrive	9
Being Human	10
Chosen	11
The One Thing	12
A World Made of Atoms	13
Something Past	14
Stories	15
The Animal in Me	16
Babylon at Night	17
The Body	18
The Mirror	19
The Places We Go To	20
Conscious	21
Begin in Abundance	22
A Little Bit of Goodness	23
He Who Waits	24
The Good Old Days	25
Close in	26
Visitors	27

LOVE 29

I Don't Mind	32
It's Us	33
Beauty's Demands	34
Backpack Love	35
No Two Hearts	37
Alone with Another	38
The Things We Love	39
Total Honesty	40
Slightly Ajar	41
An Earthly Thing	42
To Miss	43
Only Soul	44
Last Night I Dreamt	45
Friendship	47
Parents	49

SOCIETY 51

Something Above	54
Friday Night	55
The Machine	56
What Comes Next	57
Pitchfork Politics	58
Nobody to Paint	59
A Means to an End	60
Darwinian brains, Kardashian times	61
Walking By	62
Free	63
Progress	64
Humanity	65
Sometimes I See Them	66
True Belonging	67
The Lucky Ones	69
With Nothing	73

TRAVEL 75

Lucky	78
First Impressions	79
What Would It Take	80
Mexico Somewhere	81
The Last Time	83
Another World	84
These are the Days	85
Now & Never Again	87
Be Young Now	88
The World Will Wait Outside	89
Circles	91
The Second Draft	92
Home	93
In the End	94

NATURE 95

The First Time	98
The Land We Live On	99
The World is a Map	101
A Moment of Peace	102
Life Need Not Explain	103
Sacred Sunsets	105
Oh Universe	107
History Repeats	108
Water & Spirit	109

NEW WORLDS REMAIN

Beneath the Starry Sky

beneath the starry sky
that we hardly ever see

we live pondering our lives
as if a riddle to be solved

some find the answers
but the searching never ends

it takes a lifetime to know yourself
but just a moment to forget.

Other Roads

I was sick of waiting for people
I had yet to meet,
following lights
that led to darkness.

so I chose a struggle
&an explanation to match,
believing the lie
whose colours I liked.

&so with truth
as a hobby
&hope
as a plan

I walk further into the unknown
certain only
of what I do not want.

The World Grows with You

when you suffer
everyone does

when you grow
the world grows with you

there are parts of yourself
you cannot discover
let alone fulfil
on your own

the individual is necessary
but not sufficient.

But One Life

awoke
to the sound of rain
&barely an ounce of fight within.

in the ashtray,
the smouldered remains
of moments—seized
&the stubbed-out luxury
of not having to think for myself.

awoke
to the morning struggling
to renew itself
&with a dullness in my bones
I wonder...

if the future
really needs us
as much as we think it does.

sometimes beauty &meaning
are nowhere to be found—
sometimes life delivers both
all at once.

this morning I awoke
burdened

by the weight of all the things
my life could be—
&for a moment

was overcome by panic,
a steep dread
&the looming regret

that I have but
one life
to try with.

When You Arrive

there will be no certainty
or soundtrack
for the path you must walk,
for it has not yet been walked
&your footsteps are the path.

there will be no witnesses
to your most crucial moments,
for they happen within you
where your story is written

&though you will have to reduce yourself
to a mere name on paper
&then throw it into the fire
of the world

there will be no congratulations
when you arrive
where you were born to

for there will be no one worthy to do so
&you will no longer be here
to congratulate.

Being Human

the way a cup cannot hold
the ocean

the way our eyes can only know
a fraction of the landscape

the way words can never capture
the totality of an experience

the human mind will never understand
the great mystery of existence

&yet in every place we look,
the world invites us
to extend our imagination

&breathe life into the questions
only we are asked.

Chosen

like ancient mountains
we belong to the earth
&the sky

in-between creatures
of here &the heavens,
an impossible moment
with no explanation.

there is no certainty that any of this
will happen again,
nor that it matters beyond
what we decide

&yet somehow, time
has been given
asking nothing in return,

the divine gift
of expression is ours
in every moment

&we are born into lives
where we have been chosen
to remake the world
like waves on the ocean.

The One Thing

it doesn't matter
where you live,
home
is the journey itself.

we may not want to go it alone
but that is the one thing
we must do.

each morning we awake
with fear
&possibility waiting
at the foot of our bed

one says: 'don't bother. you can't'
'it's too much, too big a task'
'you couldn't possibly manage it'

the other says nothing
but waits
patiently
for the courage you possess
but have yet to discover.

A World Made of Atoms

brave the new world

where we have outrun evolution
but not our nature

where we have domesticated
the divine

&trapped ourselves in the temple
of the individual

&where we run around in circles
yet fail to close our own,

searching for wholeness
in a world made of atoms

the rational creatures
that need more than rationality.

Something Past

the body wants
beyond the flesh

a fatal race
of tiny steps

but what you want
can never last

for once it's yours
it's something past

Stories

the mind is a room
&there's dirt on the carpets

creating plots you wouldn't believe
but you go ahead anyway

thoughts sneak up
&become us

turning mood swings
into mountains

the stories that we write
end up writing us.

The Animal in Me

the animal in me
isn't happy about sharing a room
with a monk

he doesn't say it
but the monk does

they steer clear of each other
for the most part

but the monk can never find peace
constantly having to clean
the mess
the other leaves behind

things would probably be easier
if I asked one to leave
for good

the truth is
I have
many times

the animal in me
isn't happy about sharing a room
with a monk.

Babylon at Night

it's Eden in the morning
&Babylon at night
a ricochet of substances
a simple trick of light

Jesus is within me
so is Judas &the Romans
but they'll help me kick the habit
with the help of other poisons

distant as a prayer
vacant as a tomb
the game cannot be won
but always there to lose

the simplicity of substance
casts its perfect spell,
this trying to enter heaven
is a certain kind of hell.

The Body

the mind forgets
but the body keeps score
speaking in aches
we cannot ignore

a loyal servant
or a heartless dictator
bending like water
then tearing like paper

a temple of longing
a prison of spirit
our ticket to life
&ticket to exit

the mind forgets
but the body keeps score
our bridge to a world
where there isn't a door.

The Mirror

watch the surface
of yourself—point blank,
staring back in the cold
silver glass that holds you—flat
with no trace of the past
that's brought you here again,
face to face with that familiar echo
of light &skin &breath
that waits.

in the mirror
we are written like facts,
imperfections lucid
&randomly scripted,
existence scribbled
&held in an image
that answers
to the world
when we forget ourselves.

&it's just you
reduced to symmetry
&put so simply—in 2d,
a person, too deep
in the surface.

The Places We Go To

we have different bodies
but the places we go to
are the same

your aloneness—
the self-doubt
the dark thoughts
the 'if onlys'
are not beared
alone

the human psyche
has lived many lives
many times

we have different bodies
but the places we go to
are the same.

Conscious

you are not your thoughts
you are the space between them

you are not your fears
but your awareness of them

you are not your past
but your acceptance of it

the sky is always blue
it's just the clouds that have us fooled

Begin in Abundance

begin in abundance
&not from scarcity,
ask from within
&not from society

let down your defences
&be open to life
for what protects from the lows
cuts off the highs

be full in yourself
&even fuller with others
be useful to people
&the worlds you encounter

do what you fear
&discern your distractions
be kind to yourself
&honour your passions

be grateful for blessings
&the people you love
but know they belong to themselves
&never to us

receive what is given
&be free from what's taken
for there is wisdom in truth
but more in acceptance.

A Little Bit of Goodness

what a beautiful day
to live your life

what a beautiful day
to find peace with all
that is unresolved
within you

tomorrow
is a question
that answers itself

&even a little bit of goodness
is enough for today.

He Who Waits

he who waits for life
waits for death

he who cannot be happy now
may never know how

he who waits for the world
to win him back

waits too long

whatever lessons you don't learn in this life
you will have to learn
in the next.

The Good Old Days

we embraced the night
through curtains of smoke,
drinking its spells &singing its songs.

careless, uncombed &old enough,
we spoke directly
as if everything mattered
&was up to us.

we were not all from the same batch,
but we agreed on a maker,
sharing a devotion
to know ourselves suddenly
&not in the abstraction of tomorrow.

days slid into evenings
as we muddled numbness &feeling,
dismissing our bodies for the glory
within reach...

&though our songs froze time
&our laughter honoured all that was ending,
it never really dawned on us

what any of it meant,
what it would amount to when it was over,
&just how quickly a good time
can become the good old days.

Close In

life is a blessing

that can feel
like an emergency.

by design,
we live searching for truth
sturdy enough
to live by...

but life
isn't an equation;

love
doesn't yield to a spreadsheet

&even truth
is all in the timing.

you can't plan fate,
things just happen

&who can say
if it's for better or worse
when you're this close in.

Visitors

it's hard to believe
that the people you meet
are the people you lose.

that strangers
can become lovers, friends, family,
&then strangers once again

&that in each &every person
lives a protagonist—in no one's world
but their own,
destined, only
to be visitors

to meet &clash &merge
with one another
for just a moment—
often it is only a moment we share,
living silently in ourselves
in a world where nothing occurs without us
&everything is personal.

but time &time again,
what you cannot control
will disappoint you
&will do so through nothing more
than its design.

so let go
of all that is beyond you
&all that belongs
to the world of another,

revel in the motion
&measure each day
by the laughter it contains
&in meaning
&in change

for everything is fleeting
&nothing truly lost
while new worlds
still remain.

LOVE

I Don't Mind

I don't mind if you drive
I don't mind if you don't
I don't mind if you tell me what I am
&am not—I think that's the point.

you like it when I take control
&I like it when you snatch it back;
I even like it when our jokes fall flat,
for I know that nothing is perfect
&that we're both in this
together.

It's Us

it's not the world that's ending,
it's us.

it's not the years that are rushing by,
it is us who are rushing through them.

what we want is certainty
but what we are is motion

what we need is tomorrow
but what we have is today

to fall into love
is to fall into loss

to feel the weight of this life &all
that is slipping
is an impossible load

&yet when I remember the sun
&look into your eyes,
what a small price to pay

it's not the world that's ending,
it's us—
but what a small price to pay.

Beauty's Demands

memories echo like waves
in a seashell, conspiring
against the present.

stinging sweetly,
they offer warmth
&the gentle safety
of distance.

the desperate animal
of the heart—soft
&susceptible chooses
what we remember.

in moments of doubt,
memories safely lived
return to us,
soothing for a moment,
our droning questions
&trembling plots.

some memories
grow closer
with distance

some beauty demands
more than it gives.

Backpack Love

you climb atop me &I feel
like a man—until you say
it's my feminine side
that you adore.

what we have
is still barely a child,

but I know you are different
from the careful, anxious way
I craft, write
&rewrite my messages—
when so many before

have received a flurry of taps
&expiring words
that the deepest part of me
cannot own up to.

perhaps love is purest
in infancy
&in memory,
when enough—
but not all
has been revealed.

&as you close your eyes,
stealing back the worlds
hidden in your gaze

my thoughts drift
to the others
that came before

&how they could never compare
to you
or anyone else
I barely know.

No Two Hearts

love
is a false god

we are waiting
to be ruled by.

it calls by name
&calms the storm,

but no two hearts
can ever break the same.

nor love the same,
without condition

for there is no firm measure
for life's truest delusion.

Alone with Another

alone with another
alone in your sleep

the flesh is too shallow
love is too deep

words can be lies
truth can be worse

the night teaches lessons
that nobody learns.

The Things We Love

such pleasure in the things we love
but it's not pleasure we should blame
for the panic we fall into
when the feeling starts to fade

nor should we blame the nature
of the things that we adore,
but the way our fingers grip and tense
when they try to be themselves.

the Buddhists shout illusion,
but our shouts are even louder,
they do not know of rock & roll
or soul, or love forever

such madness in the things we love,
such bliss in pure reaction,
though we cannot ask each visitor
that comes to stay forever.

&if love's enough,
we will not stray far
&so we feel
it should too stay

but a flower's bloom is never lost
till we kick &shout &scream at it
to rise and live again.

Total Honesty

total honesty
no one deserves that
someone you despise maybe
not a lover
not a friend
have some decency
say nothing
change the subject
lie

Slightly Ajar

by fooling others
we fool ourselves

&yet through years
&lifetimes
a longing fills
the gaps, hiding
its subtle poison
in hope—

readying us for delusion
&for love to be willed
into tenuous being.

unconsciously
we know our depths
&pasts too well

by fooling others
we fool ourselves,

seeking to be finished
&for someone to tell us
who we are,
the heart wounded
but left slightly ajar.

An Earthly Thing

thought
is a matter of practice

it takes courage to feel
what you feel.

love
is an earthly thing,
heartbreak too—

but in joy or in sadness
we can only guess
at the work
being done within.

feeling too much
can be a burden

feeling not enough
misses the point

entirely

thought is a matter of practice
it takes courage to feel
what you feel.

To Miss

to miss someone
is to come to terms
with what it really meant

it is to be in the aching presence
of something desperate to live again—
&to truly know
what you wish you had.

to miss someone
is to sigh defenceless
into the void,

it is to be lonely
in a room
full of people

&deny the present
from having lived.

Only Soul

what draws our gaze
blinds the soul

what lights our fire
may not keep it lit.

beauty's slender truth
inspires
&convinces,

but only soul
can conquer soul.

Last Night I Dreamt

last night I dreamt
there was another
we were all there talking, laughing

he had everyone fooled,
his pretty words
his annoying air of decency

I could tell he wanted you &nothing else
I wanted to expose him,
but I couldn't
I wanted you to see
but you wouldn't listen

in the end
you chose him
&no one was surprised

I watched, helpless,
unable to look away—

&then,
just as all was lost
something warm &soft
brushed up against me

light rushed in
&I awoke to find you nestled
beside me, innocent &asleep

I wrapped my arms around you
breathed you in
&shuddered myself free

in the soft, mauve light
of the morning
I held you
pressed my face into your hair
&took none of it for granted
I'm glad the spirit is working overtime.

Friendship

friendship is the playground
where we discover who we are
&what is possible;

it is the seed
of all true belonging
&the laughter
against which
we have no defences.

a friend is both a teacher
&an admirer, emboldening
the parts of us still waiting
to announce themselves,
while subtly discouraging
what holds us back.

friendship is being seen
&accepted
time &time again,
without the pretences;

it is the water
we need to survive
&the wine which reveals
&elates us, instilling

that we are not as alone
as we often feel.

like many of life's blessings,
friendship can be felt most deeply
in its absence—

it is that gravitational pull
towards home
&the only known remedy
to the solitary nature of our lives.

friendship is our closest doorway
to meaning—without it
there would be no way
to locate ourselves
&no point in even trying.

friendship is sitting side by side
&seeing the same world
reflected back;

it is the deep &unspoken truth that says:
we need each other
&can make even the most
standard human existence
unique &extraordinary.

Parents

they are the solid ground
you walk on
&the selflessness
that asks no questions.

the way they spoke to you
became the inner voice
you have come to know
as yourself,

&though you may strive to do
what they did not,
you can never give back
what they have already given.

blame them for all
that went wrong,
if you can thank them
for all that didn't,

&for all that was left open
for you to decide;

for we may inherit their virtues,
but it is the unique parts
of us—the ones

that are wholly ours
that are their greatest triumph.

they are the seeds, the soil
&the labour of the harvest
that is your life;

they are the love
that was pure enough
to sacrifice everything
&then let you go.

SOCIETY

Something Above

faith's out of fashion
&God is a lie,
a material age
of spiritual guides

who give us the answers
but just for a moment,
for the meaning of life
is part of their business.

&so we keep looking
&searching &scrolling,
living our lives
like nobody's watching

&with the devil below
pray there's something above,
but if God's really watching
he probably fears us.

Friday Night

lights, voices
&naked
without a glass to hold

shoulders fight to loosen
beneath a tired routine
&a trembling
hardness.

alcohol helps to numb
but still he teeters
always
on the unspeakable.

danger hums
drones
for him
&those he loves

for there is nothing
more fragile
than a man

who half-knows
what he's not.

The Machine

work for it
&it will keep you safe

give yourself to it
&it will fulfill your every desire
but leave you always wanting more

try to leave it
&it will ask where you're going
&give you a thousand reasons to stay

will you miss it?
in some ways, of course.

will it miss you?
not for a second.

What Comes Next

America was great
democracy was fun
but at some point
you've got to stop making excuses

our precious economy
running empty
our sacred institutions
are there any left

what used to happen in back alleys
now happens on the main street

America was great
democracy was fun
what comes next

Pitchfork Politics

a war is waged from either side
of the line where we belong,
hatred is our currency
disgust our uniform

I draw my strength from weakness
you pretend that you're still strong,
I cling to my deepest fears
lest they're proven wrong

you don't want the world to burn
I think it's burning now,
you want to tell me what to love
I want to show you how

bodies lie torn &shamed
where there used to be a middle,
I want the world to grow
you want it to stay simple

in another world we're brothers
in another world, of course
in another world the curtain burns
&the narrative falls short

for this war is nothing new
&there are those who know this well,
those who rule in silence
while we fight amongst ourselves.

Nobody to Paint

speak coldly of humanity
but boldly of its people,
for who can blame the creatures
that live beneath these waters

speak plainly of the end times
while the party rages on,
does a river merely flow
the way it wants to go

perhaps a day will come
when lions roam
through city streets,

when the last war has been fought
&the last light flickers out
&dies

&finally, after all this,
there will be nothing left
but the animals,
our ruins
&nobody to paint them.

A Means to an End

we all have our dreams
but existence isn't cheap
so we try to squeeze our lives
into two days a week

each day another stepping stone
to the day where we can rest,
treating entire years
as a means to an end.

we suffer towards our goals
without thinking of the cost,
taking breaks to recharge
while thinking *only* of the cost

but this is what you've gotta do
&this is how it has to be,
save your dreams for when you sleep
because existence isn't cheap.

Darwinian brains, Kardashian times

Darwinian brains, Kardashian times
where everything's fucked,
but everything's fine

where your bank is the first
to say Happy Birthday,
where we're moving to Mars
&betting on doomsday

selling your soul is playing it safe
generosity's risky &lowers your wage,
evil agendas enlist the brightest of minds,
just supply &demand, these are the times

civilisation's falling but insisting it's flying,
depressed millionaires &insecure tyrants,
highly evolved with illusions to match
but whatever your problem,
there's a Ted Talk for that!

busy's the game &freedom's the prize
yet most of us play till the day that we die
but things will be fine—
it's not as bad as you think
I, for one, believe in the world
after a couple of drinks.

Walking By

their strides align
the tension rises,
one steals a glance
then eyes the pavement.

steps are quickened,
conviction feigned,
their gazes scour
over sunken grooves.

panicked thoughts—
just keep on walking,
a simple greeting?
is it *still* morning?

am I anxious?
or are they the weird one?
two people pass
in painful silence.

Free

I sold my time
for money

hoping
I would be able to buy some of it back later

but the price went up
so I never did.

I'd like to do it over
but maybe it would be worse

I'd like to be free
but I don't remember how

Progress

progress is eight billion protagonists
progress is longer lives & longer hours
progress is texting while driving
progress is a thousand ways to cook an egg

progress is Donald Trump & Kanye West
progress is teenage crypto-billionaires
progress breaks down barriers
&builds new ones
progress is the mess we're in

progress is talking about the problem
progress is the luxury of talking about the problem
progress has started more wars
than it can count
progress is one side of the story

Humanity

humanity
is the winning streak

nature
wasn't ready for

it hasn't been pretty
or peaceful

but you can't say
we have nothing

to show for it

Sometimes I See Them

shoulder to shoulder on metal racks,
a press of bodies tighten &sway
to the violence of the evening bus.

people close their eyes to get home faster
&cannot remember what they signed
or when.

sometimes I see them,
sometimes I don't.

sometimes I look into their faces
&feel nothing

sometimes I feel our secrets
are not all that different.

a boy in headphones fervently tapping
fingers on thighs

a tired mother clutching the seat
with one hand while soothing
her baby in the other

an old man keeping on for the occasional
glimpse of the few still left.

sometimes I see them,
sometimes I don't.

True Belonging

Australia,
I wish loving you
was simpler

I wish my freedom
did not come at a price
I never agreed to pay

I wish the words
'home' & 'country'
were rightfully ours

&that my blessings
weren't ripped
from innocent hands

&I wish
that you would see all this...

&be open
&willing

the way I know
you could be.

I wish these things
because I do love you

but a shadow hangs over all
you have given me

&I cannot embrace
the denial
that true belonging
demands.

The Lucky Ones

a swell of bodies emerge
from beneath the city,
a sea of shoulders &bags spilling
onto the sidewalk.

people jostle by, hurried
by the fading light,
disguised in their uniforms
&purposeful strides,
sober faces like painted masks.

headphoned &stifled together,
we march in a consensus
of grownupness.

I weave in and amongst them,
following anxious eyes darting
around like fish in a tank,
barely resting on anything
long enough to see it.

we move separately—as one
through gauntlets of advertising
&suffocating car horns, swelling forward
like some great migration

of a species adaptable
to any kind of madness;

people surge &scan anxiously
for their buses, enduring the fumes
&facing all that evolution
&high school
never prepared us for.

lights change
&we rush forward again,
desperate to get home
&salvage what little remains.

an unexpected thud
finds my shoulder—the scrunched face
of a middle-aged woman looking
at me through sunken eyes
as if I am all the ills of society,
cursing me &whichever group I belong to.

I push on, silently mumbling
my own curses.

up ahead sits a cardboard abode
&its homeless man, dishevelled

&easy to miss in his murky shades
of grey &brown fraying
at every opportunity.

as I approach to pass him
he catches my gaze
with surprising, lingering green eyes

&tells me
in a bedraggled smile
not to waste all of my good despair
while I am still so young.

I feel a pang of guilt—
but am suddenly distracted
by the sight of a well-dressed man eating
something I have not—
&then by the rising clamour of voices,
another wave of bodies
being issued towards me
from beneath the ground,

&as I pass
&forget him
in the same step,
I feel that familiar, dreaded weight,

a sudden helplessness—titantic,
of some impossible obstacle,
of not knowing which direction to go,
of all that is not yet real
but always approaching
with every step
I do not take.

is this really all there is?
who does all this belong to?
is this the engine or the carriage?

which of us are the lucky ones?

perhaps these questions
are a waste of time.

perhaps there has never been a world
that was up to the people.

With Nothing

the sun rises
&the lights come on
&everyone plays their game
&we all get on
for better or worse.

mistakes are made,
hearts are promised,
lives are lived
&it's fun
&important
for a while.

but in the end,
we all go home
with nothing—back
to that infinite place
where I am you
&you are me.

TRAVEL

Lucky

start over
in every city

awake
to unfamiliar faces
&spin around like the arrow
on your map
to find a place
you've never been.

sunburnt travellers weave
through crowded streets,
burdened by ticking end dates
&carpe diem.

perfectly idle moments come &go
without warning, soaking us
in a luxury the rich
cannot afford.

places wonder who we are,
why we came
&where we're going

I guess we are lucky enough
not to know.

First Impressions

unpack again alone
in a room with 12 beds.

search through bags of cold,
tired clothing to find the same
worn outfit that never gets old
to new faces.

first impressions reveal
almost nothing,
or hatch entire futures,
if you're looking.

What Would It Take

with nothing in common
but a time &place
we sit side by side,
starting from scratch.

familiar questions
find familiar responses
that smooth &shroud
the clumsy, desperate parts.

I say something I've said before
then ask you what you're reading
&if you have plans for later

I want to ask...

what was the time
of your life?

what would it take
for this to be it?

Mexico Somewhere

tired zippers beg for mercy
eyes search for gaps where bags can rest
candy-coloured colonial buildings
pawing vendors do their duty

shops selling identical stock
markets selling identical shops
broken English the universal language
festive music forgets the past

indigenous threads cling to sweat &freckles
gawking eyes follow blue-eyed giants
cities nourished on ancient ruins
cameras capture all they can

violent clangs of church bells wander
voice messages from distant lands
children glow with youth &laughter
leathered women move pavement dust

family dinners with total strangers
ask for less &then for more
slurred mezcal invitations
careless comments like javelins thrown

sunburnt mood swings arrive in stillness
journal scribbles calm themselves
smiling faces, answered questions
another day you won't remember

podcast dinners, empty dorms
home is people, smells &buses
cracks mapped on dirty pavements
booked tickets weigh like luggage

conversations with unsaved numbers
time means nothing without a friend
passing travellers flash worlds with glances
too many lives to really live any.

The Last Time

everything you do today
you will one day do

for the last time.

normal
is a blessing

we never know
until it's too late;

solid ground
is the great illusion
of our time

&in every moment
a golden age is revealed
in its ending.

Another World

plant roots
with plans to leave

another world
another time

another name
you won't remember

another face
that isn't hers

a new beginning
another plan

keep moving
to keep forgetting

These are the Days

sunlit clouds stay in their lanes
&sail across an ocean of sky.

up above, an unbearable fiery
medallion throned in the distant blue,
paints the day in a lustrous, sleepy haze.

we met by chance
&were strangers for barely a moment,
honouring ourselves
&the time we did not have.

before us rolling hills swell &climb
into hulking mountains—indifferent
to the cratered purring
of the city below.

back &forth we reveal ourselves,
quickly discovering who we are
&would not be.

atop a grassy landing
we bathe in the sun's opiate rays,
allowing ourselves to be wrapped in the
warm, smug embrace
of an unearned spring.

from time to time we say whatever
is on our minds, our limbs stretching
out nostalgically for something
too far away to reach...

high above, lumbering clouds move
with simpler destinies, mocking us
with their slow, mindless obedience.

the smell of altitude
&freshly cut grass passes over,
&absently,
in the lethargic endlessness of the day,
we lie and witness the view
we awoke to—ignorant, elsewhere victims
to the inescapable subtlety
of bliss.

these are the days
that will know their worth
when they belong to another life.

these are the days we will cherish
when we are old
&unable to remember
how we really felt.

Now & Never Again

life isn't short—there's nothing longer,
but we do ourselves no favours
with our grand measures of time.

a week vanishes without a trace,
months reduce to a few scattered memories
&the year rushes to be over,
building decades that we will one day
look back on as something
that simply occurred.

in the world of calendars—months, years,
goals &plans, life passes...
but its true essence
is lived in seconds,
in infinitesimal moments of presence
&single breaths.

civilisations last a thousand years,
mountains rise &fall
to the rhythm of centuries,
&yet nothing occurs
outside of a moment,

&the reality of your life
is always
now
&never again.

Be Young Now

growing up will get you
in the end.

whether you follow your dreams
or play it safe—life
catches up
one way or another

so roll the dice as many times
as it takes—be young now

growing up will get you
in the end.

The World Will Wait Outside

come and dance in the palm of my hand,
the world will wait outside.

you sang the words
as if they could be your last.

we let go like children,
rambling leaps &bounds,
midnight at our heels, giddy to be alive
&wearing the disguise of age.

it was never a question of what we deserved,
nor perfection; we merely wanted
something close to what we had once
glimpsed was possible.

you spoke of the world as if
you were not a part of it—outrage
at arm's length, compelling me to recall
long-forgotten convictions
&abandon those I could not remember...
neither of us knows what the world needs
so we harp on what it doesn't.

perhaps a lifetime is not such an impossible
distance to delude yourself—to pretend that
we are actually capable of living up

to your lofty ideal—unconditional love
something you mention casually as if
it didn't require anything more
than our nature.

what you did that evening
with that tiny, haplessly acrylic'd guitar
is more than what some poets do in their
entirety.

melody sings the ineffable—magic even
to magicians, deeper than feeling &better
than knowing, capturing all that words
can merely gesture towards.

I imagine that's how songs are written
where you're from, ethereal
&in a single, painless stroke,
unbridled by knowledge or effort

&now, for as long as I can imagine
those three gentle shapes—
those simple chords which practically
strummed themselves
will return me to you
&the fact that someone out there,
is dancing, happily,
in the palm of your hand,
while the world waits outside.

Circles

for years
I have walked,
waiting
to arrive

wondering
if anyone does...

an entire lifetime
spent pressing
forward—&yet
I have been here before

I can only hope
these circles
are growing larger.

The Second Draft

you are not so wrong
as to not be forgiven

you are not so lost
as to not find your way back

it is not too late to find out
what really drives you—

to ask yourself
if you really want to go
where this path is leading

without that courageous first step—
the one
you have yet to take,

the way you came
becomes the way you go

sometimes the second draft
must be written
with the ashes
of the first.

Home

arrived home
to where the sky seems bigger
than anywhere else

to where wilderness abounds
&people live in the gaps;

to a country nourished
by a brutal past,

where we now enjoy the luxury
of tossing the coin
until it's right.

arrived home
to a country I wasn't born in

but has humbled me
with the knowing

that all that I am is nothing
compared
to what I've been given.

In the End

there isn't time to see
the whole world

there's barely time to see
where we are now

we were meant
to wander—to grow
&meet ourselves
in new places;

movement keeps us light
&change stretches the days

but in the end we hope to find
something
to hold us down.

NATURE

The First Time

knowledge feeds the mind
as wonder feeds the soul
&so I keep close &am sustained
by that which can be glimpsed
in the night sky;

by the miracles we depend on
but don't understand—the mysterious
hidden world of processes
that architects mountains &paints sunsets
never the same twice,

that turns water &sunlight
into fruit
&heartache into music,
that lets two beating hearts join
to become three

&that allows consciousness to arise
in a universe made of matter—
even atoms must be amazed
at what they accomplish.

through us the mystery comes alive
through us the universe
is given new eyes to see itself
for the first time.

The Land We Live On

in a single patch
of bushland
nature is itself
in a million different ways.

mighty eucalypts,
like living monoliths, rise
with a silent sentience,
each finding its own path
towards the heavens.

every leaf—novel
&yet complete
in itself, sprouts only

to wither &return
to the forest floor—death
resting upon a bed of life.

great families of trees whisper
wordless secrets in the breeze,
as kookaburras join
the laughter of the river,
honouring a joke
as old as time itself.

the Australian landscape
is an ancient dream
the earth is having;

it is a land where people have roamed
since there were people

a land whose original custodians knew
belonged entirely to itself,

offering us a wisdom
not learned
but remembered.

The World is a Map

the world is a map
to the eagle
&the dreamer,
who sees mountains as hills
&the sky as a witness.

rivers &trails are the veins
of their kingdom
&oceans are streams
to cross &defy

&though the eagle &the dreamer fly
as if it all belonged to them,
somehow they know
they are at the centre
of nothing

&that every creature carries
the truth in its eye
&the world
in its mind.

A Moment of Peace

shoes on my hands
moss on my feet
resisting the flow
that barrels downstream

thinking of nothing
but the icy below
the feeling of rocks
the grip of my toes

world in the distance
sun in the trees
fish out of water
high on the breeze

gripped by the current
a moment of peace
shoes on my hands
moss on my feet

Life Need Not Explain

behind the rush of light &sound,
behind the veil of thought
is a faint humming,
a steady whispering
reminding us

that we are not here for nearly as long
as love or drugs would have us believe,
&that this stirring passage—
this vivid whirling of colour &spirit
may well be heaven
or the closest thing that exists.

for in a sea of suffocating darkness,
upon a mysterious drop
of unlikely blue, the imagination
is humbled—&somehow...

love exists
against all odds—
life is a fact
with no explanation

&we are given the chance
to express what we are
&be more than we're made of
in every moment.

&yet in all of life's endless poetry,
inhaled with every breath,
there is an aching within us for purpose

an ancient restlessness for reason
&meaning—for an author's account
to the age-old questions
that keep us painfully human.

but if what they say is true,
if all that came before this
was sheer blackness, empty space
&expressionless silence,
then life need not explain itself
for surely it has done enough

in raising spirit from dust,
in sourcing light from darkness,
&turning zero to one.

so perhaps it is our turn
to explain, &it is life
that is waiting
for us
to live
as the reason,
to give this lucid gasp its meaning
&to answer boldly
why it is we are here.

Sacred Sunsets

sacred sunsets
invent new oranges,
teaching us new heights
&other things
we don't understand.

fiery alien shades—nameless
&incapable of repetition, blend
&find seamless union,
illuminating regal bursts of clouds,
billowing like smoke
yet holding perfect form.

like a spell
the world slows into clarity
as nature's ephemeral strokes
sink us into ourselves,
leaving us to wonder

where
the inspiration
for such works come from

&Who
we have to thank
for these bold, fleeting creations.

maybe when all this is over
&we are dust
&boring once more
someone will fill us in on
why we felt the way we did

&the reason behind those perfect,
fading oranges
that stir &humble
the silent animal within.

Oh Universe

oh Universe,
great open sky,
God, if I must

let my mind be an instrument
for something greater
than itself

let my body serve a higher purpose
than it already has

allow me to hear
what my soul has whispered
all along

&let my life be a song
where you practice some new melody
even you
have never heard.

History Repeats

history repeats
&the price is always rising,
the fate of the world depends
on the mood of the biosphere

it rests upon the things that we do
when we're comfortable
&on the whims of a universe
that maybe isn't listening.

the music's slowly fading,
but the party keeps raging
while the ice blocks melt
in the glasses that we clink

ancient days approaching
as the earth grows violent,
history repeats
&the price is always rising.

Water & Spirit

we are water &spirit
in disposable cups,
pouring ourselves back
into the ocean

but from the moment we're born
we begin to forget this,
given names &a culture
&language that writes us,

we inherit our instincts,
get beliefs in an instant
&learn to worship a God
we have tamed with a word
&caged in our image.

for somewhere along the path
we strayed from our nature,
seeing ourselves separate
to the surroundings that raised us

we traded wisdom for knowledge
&wrote history through conquest,
mistaking violence for glory
&movement for progress.

but for everything gained
something is lost,

&for all our advances
&attempts to transcend—
eternal facts endure.

the essence of what we are
remains unchanged;
the place we came from &will return to
is no different,
&we remain an open question
with no clear answer—wandering echoes
of the same noise,

mysterious notes in a greater symphony—
water &spirit in disposable cups
momentarily witnessed by the sun &the sky.

&somehow, in this unlikely lucid flash,
we begin each day anew, living
in a world where time favours
no single moment over any other,

offering existence in each breath
&the chance to become what we are
in every moment,
creating ripples &impressions
that last forever,
as we pour ourselves, slowly,
back
into the ocean.

50% of all profits from this book are donated to the Fred Hollows Foundation - An international organisation working towards eliminating avoidable blindness & improving Indigenous Australian health.

ACKNOWLEDGEMENTS

Thank you to all the people who helped make this book possible, particularly my parents, my partner and my close friends and family, whose love, generosity and unwavering support made all the difference.

Thanks For Reading

If you enjoyed this book, let me know via
Instagram or at flashpoetryproject@gmail.com
All messages/feedback are greatly appreciated
and will act as fuel for the next project.

You can also help out by sharing this book with
anyone you think might like it. Without traditional
marketing, this book relies on word-of-mouth
and readers like you to help get it out there.

Thank you for your time. I thoroughly enjoyed
writing each & every poem in this book,
and I hope you enjoyed reading them.

For more poetry, visit:

 @_flashpoetry

www.ingramcontent.com/pod-product-compliance
Lightning Source LLC
Chambersburg PA
CBHW020325010526
44107CB00054B/1988